LEVITY

by

Lewis Karstensson

DORRANCE
PUBLISHING CO
EST. 1920
PITTSBURGH, PENNSYLVANIA 15238

Dorrance Publishing Co.
585 Alpha Drive
Suite 103
Pittsburgh, PA 15238

Visit our website at www.dorrancebookstore.com

ISBN: 978-1-4809-4223-3
eISBN: 978-1-4809-4200-4

Preface

My sedentary retirement, off the golf course, is largely sedentary. But then I like sedentary. It is mostly spent in reading the classics of Cervantes, Dickens, Molière, Steinbeck, Twain, Voltaire and the like, and watching old TV shows, like *Paladin*, *Cheers*, and *M*A*S*H*. However, my small mind also occasionally wanders into the realm of memory where I find myself laughing at some of the adventures and misadventures in and around my youth. I have committed a few of these memories to paper in order to retrieve these laughs at will. There too may be a remote possibility that a distant descendent might also have a laugh.

So this slight volume is a collection of these memories. The initial item is my family studbook. It suggests little more than that my ancestry is dry, a blend of ten parts farming, one part music, no olives. Items two through six are stories involving my father, my two sisters, and myself. Here we find my dad in the company of a mischievous Swedish expatriate, my sisters decidedly independent, and me having a slight creative streak in spite, or perhaps because, of a brain disorder. Items seven through twelve recount some hunting adventures with friends. These friends were always leading me astray, into all manner of trouble. And item thirteen is an account of a recent conversation between two old sterile adolescents about an illegal angling innovation of little importance or not.

This product comes with no warranty. It is my hope, however, that the reader finds a laugh or two in these little excursions into levity.

CONTENTS

The church is near but the road is icy;
the bar is far away but I'll walk carefully.

Russian Proverb

LEVITY

If you cannot get rid of the family skeleton,
you may as well make it dance.

George Bernard Shaw
Immaturity (1931)

1. THE FAMILY

G enealogy, rummaging through the records of dead people in search of roots to a family tree, is not a recreation on which I wish to spend much time. It is rather equivalent to assembling one of those 1,500-piece jigsaw puzzles of a totally blue sky. I, however, am willing to devote a little energy to retelling the work of others about our family lineage. So this short article is the result of my effort to put together an inventory of the members of the Karstensson clan to the limited extent that such a list is possible. I had hoped to trace our lineage back to someone important like Gustav Vasa or Queen Christina, but, alas, it was only traceable to a Danish protestant priest.

The article has three parts. The first section presents some of the ancestry of my father, Hans Karstensson (1896-1992). This part draws heavily on documents provided by Lennart Nilsson of Borgeby, Skåne, Sweden. The second section presents a bit of the ancestry of my mother, Iris Almeda Smith (1905-1989). This part rests largely on her genealogy papers. And the third section summarizes the descendants of Hans Karstensson and Iris Almeda Smith Karstensson. Much of this information was forced from the living, by the author, in e-mails and phone conversations. The particular disparate sources are listed at the end of the piece.

And a final notational note. Numbers signify different generations in a series; na means not available; and c means approximately. Numbers are also used to identify specific farms in Skåne, Sweden; Veberöd 25, for example, refers to farm 25 in Veberöd.

Ancestry of Hans Karstensson

1. Carsten Clow: b. 1622; d. 1700. Maria Gerdes: b. 1630; d. 1707. Carsten was born in Tønder, Syddanmark, Denmark; studied for the priesthood at Copenhagen University; became a military priest (protestant denomination), chaplain, in Malmö, Skåne, Sweden in 1658; became a parish priest in Röddinge-Ramsåsa, Skåne, Sweden in 1667; died in Röddinge, Skåne, Sweden.

2. Christopher Carstensson Clow: b. 1660; d. 1709. Adela Pedersdotter: b. 1660; d. 1718. Christopher was a forester; had a farm at Veberöd, Skåne, Sweden.

3. Mathias Christoffersson Clow: b. 1696; d. 1728. Metta Knutsdotter: b. 1697; d. 1742. Mathias was second lieutenant in the cavalry; had a farm at Veberöd.

4. Knut Mathiasson Clow: b. 1722; d. 1792. Elna Jönsdotter: b. 1730; d. 1794. Knut was a farmer at Veberöd.

5. Mathias Knutsson: b. 1765; d. 1818. Sissa Andesdotter: b. 1774; d. 1851. Mathias was a farmer at Veberöd.

6. Carsten Mathiasson: b. 4/22/1804 Veberöd 25, Almelund, Veberöd; d. 1849 Hällestad, Skåne, Sweden. Margareta Nilsdotter: b. 8/7/1809 St. Rodde, Everlöv; d. 7/6/1876 Hällestad 4, Hällestad. Carsten was a farmer at Hällestad.

7. Jöns Carstensson: b. 4/29/1834 Hällestad 4, Hällestad; d. 9/16/1899 Hällestad 4, Hällestad. Bengta Hansdotter: b. 8/18/1837 Södra Sandby; d. 11/19/1917 Hällestad 4, Hällestad. Marriage: 12/27/1856 Södra Sandby. Children: Bengta Jönsdotter: b. 6/18/1857; d. 12/26/1929. Hans Jönsson: b. 3/19/1862; d. 2/8/1902. Carsten Jönsson: b. 2/15/1867; d. 2/17/1932. Elna Jönsdotter: b. 8/18/1869; d. 8/12/1934. Jöns was a farmer at Hällestad.

8. Hans Jönsson: b. 3/19/1862 Hällestad 4, Hällestad; d. 2/8/1902 Västra Tvet, Hällestad. Karna Svensdotter: b. 8/1/1861 Sjöstorp 2, Dalby; d. 7/24/1913 Västra Tvet, Hällestad. Marriage: 6/9/1886. Children: Nils Anton Carstensson: b. 4/20/1887 Dalby; d. 12/5/1910 Västra Tvet, Hällestad. Selma Marie Carstensson Nilsson: b. 4/26/1889 Dalby; d. 4/3/1977 Vänersborg. Clara Amanda Carstensson Gustafsson: b. 4/28/1892 Västra Tvet, Hällestad; d. 3/9/1981 Floda. Hans Carstensson Karstensson: b. 11/14/1896 Västra Tvet, Hällestad; d. 9/1/1992 Las Vegas, Nevada. Hans Jönsson was a farmer at Västra Tvet, Hällestad.

Ancestry of Iris Almeda Smith

1.1 Josiah Thompson Smith: b. na; d. na. Nancy Cummings: b.1812; d. 1894. Marriage: na. Children: James Milton Smith. Natives of Pennsylvania and Ohio respectively; moved to Burlington, Iowa in 1839 or 1840.

1.2 David H. Davis: b. na; d. na. Mary Jane Davis: b. na; d. na. Marriage: na. Children: Lucinda Davis.

2.1 James Milton Smith: b. 9/20/1835 Hamilton County, Ohio; d. 9/16/1914 Etna, California. Lucinda Davis: b. 6/20/1855 Scott Valley, California; d. 6/19/1948 Etna, California. Marriage: 12/7/1873. Children: Lucius Milton Smith. Frank Earnest Smith. In 1859 James Milton moved from Burlington, Iowa to Crystal Creek, California (a pioneer settlement some two miles north of the current town of Etna) and then later to Etna Mills, California. He was Postmaster in Crystal Creek; established and operated a wagon and carpenter shop; and was a musician who gave lessons on many instruments (including violin and organ) and conducted and played in several bands. Interested in harvesting grain, he invented the "Challenge Thresher," patented on November 3, 1855 (or 1885?). Lucinda Davis claimed to be the first white girl born in Scott Valley.

2.2 Lewis Edgar Hughes: b. 5/26/1822; d. 10/16/1907 Hughes Ranch in Scott Valley, California. Christina Eller: b. 1/29/1843 Indiana; d. 11/28/1919 Etna, California. Marriage: c. 1867. Children: Eliza Jane Hughes Eaton. John Hughes. Ralph Hughes. Aron Edgar Hughes: b. 8/11/1871 Etna, California; d. 11/30/1947 Yreka, California. Susie Hughes: b. 12/16/1875; d. 9/19/1963. Lewis Edgar was a native of Jackson County, Ohio. Came west in c. 1853 and settled on the Hughes Ranch near Rough & Ready (Etna Mills), California. Went back east in 1867 and returned with his bride, Christina Eller, in the Spring of 1868 via the Isthmus of Panama. Christina Eller was a native of Hagerstown, Indiana.

3.1 Lucius Milton Smith: b. 8/28/1874 Etna, California; d. 6/25/1944. Susie Hughes: b. 12/16/1875 Hughes Ranch in Scott Valley, California; d. 9/19/1963. Marriage: 10/27/1898. Children: Carl V. Smith: b. na; d. na. Lewis Everett Smith: b. 1901; d. 7/30/1918. Hazel Zelma Smith Carrier: b. 1904; d. 1995. Iris Almeda Smith Karstensson: b. 11/14/1905; d. 6/8/1989. Verna Smith Farnsworth: b. 1908; d. 1981. Chester A. Smith: b. 2/29/1912; d. 7/7/1977. Infant Daughter: d. 8/29/1916. Ernest Clifton Smith: b. 10/6/1917; d. 11/24/1999. Velma Christina (Toby) Smith Lincoln: b. 4/27/1920; d. na. Lucius Milton and his brother, Frank Earnest, worked with their father. They were also musicians who played with various bands and orchestras; Lucius Milton played the baritone and violin while Frank Earnest played the coronet. Frank, for a time, played with the John Philip Sousa Band. In his later years, Lucius Milton worked in farm labor, county road work, and his final employment was with the United States Forest Service in the Klamath National Forest.

Descendants of Hans and Iris Karstensson

1. Hans Karstensson: b. 11/14/1896 Västra Tvet, Hällestad; d. 9/1/1992 Las Vegas, Nevada. Iris Almeda Smith: b. 11/14/1905 Etna, California; d. 6/8/1989 Yreka, California. Marriage: 5/13/1933. Children: Verna Rae Koepp Karstensson Hance. Karna Karstensson Conrad. Lewis Karstensson. Hans Karstensson was a dairy supervisor for the Edson-Foulke Company in Gazelle, California, and a program administrator for the United States Department of Agriculture in Siskiyou County, California. Iris Karstensson was a homemaker, office employee with the City of Yreka, and bookkeeper for Dr. Ralph Schlappi, a Yreka physician.

2.1 Verna Rae Koepp Karstensson: b. 4/25/1925; d. 12/12/1994. Daughter of Iris Almeda Smith by a previous marriage. Verna Rae had a child with a man named Willard Thomas Hance. Child: Leslie Susan Hance. Verna Rae Hance was an executive stenographer.

2.2 Karna Karstensson: b. 7/11/1934 McCloud, California; d. 8/31/1995 Santa Clara, California. Gerald Henry Conrad Sr.: b. 4/30/1927; d. 11/5/1998. Marriage: 1956. Children: Kaarin Lewise Conrad Hedberg. Gerald Henry Conrad, Jr. Karna Karstensson Conrad was a homemaker and secondary school teacher. Gerald Conrad Sr. was an automobile salesman, Postmaster in Yreka, California, bookkeeper, and volunteer fireman.

2.3 Lewis Karstensson: b. 10/14/1939 McCloud, California. Kathleen Ann Barta: b. 9/1/1943. Marriage: 6/17/1967 Steele, North Dakota. Children: Kristina Karstensson Edwards. Linne Karstensson DePasquale. Lewis Karstensson is a retired professor of economics. Kathleen Karstensson is a retired secondary school teacher.

3.1 Leslie Susan Hance: b. 1/17/1957.

3.2 Kaarin Lewise Conrad: b. 10/8/1958. James Gordan Hedberg: b. 1/23/1960. Marriage: 3/30/1985. Children: Erik James Hedberg, Kristofer Hans Hedberg.

3.3 Gerald Henry Conrad, Jr.: b. 8/22/1960; d. 3/6/2014. Wife 1: Laura: b. na. Marriage: c. 1980. Child: Josh Michael Conrad. Wife 2: Carey: b. na. Marriage: 6/16/1991. Children: Kimberley Michelle Conrad. Andrew James Conrad.

3.4 Kristina Karstensson: b. 7/21/1975. Ryan Michael Edwards: b. 11/24/1972. Marriage: 9/17/2005. Children: Emmerson Grayce Edwards. Owen Layne Edwards.

3.5 Linne Karstensson: b. 12/10/1981. Anthony DePasquale III: b. 1/1/1979. Marriage: 5/25/2008. Children: Anthony Everett DePasquale IV. Calia Esther DePasquale.

4.1 Erik James Hedberg: b. 1/1/1989.

4.2 Kristofer Hans Hedberg: b. 5/29/1991.

4.3 Josh Michael Conrad: b. 10/1/1980.

4.4 Kimberley Michelle Conrad: b. na.

4.5 Andrew James Conrad: b. 3/3/1996.

4.6 Emmerson Grayce Edwards: b. 10/3/2006.

4.7 Owen Layne Edwards: b. 12/15/2008.

4.8 Anthony Everett DePasquale IV: b. 8/21/2016.

4.9 Calia Esther DePasquale: b. 8/21/2016.

Sources

1. Kathy Graves, "Etna Bands," *The Siskiyou Pioneer: The Old Brass and Town Bands of Siskiyou County* (Vol. 9, No. 3, 2013), pp. 40-49.

2. Kathy Graves, "J. Milton Smith," *The Siskiyou Pioneer: The Old Brass and Town Bands of Siskiyou County* (Vol. 9, No. 3, 2013), pp. 112-114.

3. Iris Smith Karstensson, "Early Residents of Scott Valley, Siskiyou County, California" (Yreka, California: May 8, 1973, unpublished paper).

4. Lennart Nilsson, "The relations between the cousins Ida and Hans and the Clow family" (Borgeby: April 19, 2016).

5. "Personakt, Åbo Jöns Carstensson" (February 2, 2016).

6. "Personakt, Åbo Hans Jönsson" (December 16, 2015).

7. "Personakt, Hans Karstensson f. Carstensson" (January 2, 2016).

8. Personal interviews via phone conversation and e-mail by the author with Sue Hance, Kaarin Hedberg, Kristina Edwards, and Linne DePasquale.

If the museums of the region are to be believed,
most prehistoric Scandinavians spent their lives trudging, alone,
across windswept heaths before accidentally falling into peat bogs and dying.

Michael Booth
The Almost Nearly Perfect People (2014)

2. TWO SONS OF SKÅNE*

Skåne landskap is barely in Sweden, on its southern tip. It is naturally sep-
arated from Denmark by the Øresund Strait between the two countries.
However, the lands were reconnected in 2000 by the Øresundsbroen, the
Danish bridge, or the Öresundsbron, the Swedish bridge, linking Copenhagen and Malmö.

The province is important for its agriculture. It is Sweden's granary largely
because the growing season is longer here than in the more northern provinces
in and around the Arctic Circle. However, another important feature of Skåne,
rarely noticed outside Minnesota, is the export of its youth. And numbered
among its early twentieth century exports were one Nils Nilsson and a Hans
Karstensson. This piece is an occasion to notice these progeny of Skåne for
their modest contributions to Nordic civilization, almost worth remembering.

Nils Nilsson

Nils Nilsson was the son of Anders Nilsson and Ida Svensson. They had
the farm, Lilla Bjällerup, Bostället, a short distance west of Dalby. This is
where Nils was raised.

Lore holds that when the young man approached adulthood, Anders, the
father, gave Nils, the son, a one-way ticket to Madagascar! The reason? The
father had had enough of the pranks and vocational dreams of the son. Nils

*This account benefitted from information and suggestions provided by Claes Nils-
son and Lennart Nilsson.

and Hans, once removed first cousins, were mischievous friends whose favorite after-school recreation was to harass local police by repeatedly parading heavy timbers, lifted from construction sites, around town. Then at family gatherings like christenings, weddings, and funerals the two would go off by themselves and place heavy logs or timbers across roads and railroads so as to impede travel and raise family ire. And the last straw for the father was Nils's expressed interest in flying and, to this end, joining the Swedish Air Force. The elder suspected this line of work would not provide income sufficient to support the son's accustomed level of living, and he, the father, was not about to subsidize the airy venture. The solution was to send the kid to Madagascar, with the not-so-subtle hint of no return fare.

So off to Madagascar Nils went in 1923. What he did on the island, and how long he stayed there, are lost details. However, it is known that he ended up in South Africa, where he migrated from location to location and from job to job. He alternately lived in Hermanus and Cape Town on the south coast, and then inland in Johannesburg. And he was variously police-man, farmer, miner, diamond merchant, and hôtelier. It is highly likely his underlying interest was that of accumulating cash sufficient for occasional trips to the French Riviera and Monte Carlo, for rest and recreation, until the money ran out!

It surely would not be in character for Nils to flout the wishes of his father. And yet he did make return trips to Skåne in 1929 and 1954, but apparently only for brief visits.

Hans Karstensson

Hans Karstensson, born Carstensson but changed to Karstensson for some mys-terious, perhaps nefarious, reason was the son of Hans Jönsson and Karna Svensson. They had the estate, Västra Tvet, Hällestad, just east of Dalby. This is where Hans grew up.

Now young Hans might have been forcibly deported like Nils, but his cir-cumstances were different. His father died when he was just five years old; his older brother, Nils Anton, passed away when he was fourteen; and his mother expired when he was seventeen. There were no adults left alive in the family to expel him. Then, shortly after the mother's death, his two older sisters, Selma and Clara, sold the estate for 127,000 kr. With most of his relatives gone and the farm no longer in the family, there was no reason to stay in Skåne. After spending some three years attending various agricultural schools in other provinces in Sweden, Hans went to the United States. He spent the 1922-23 academic year taking agriculture and English courses at Purdue University, and partying with his Cosmopolitan Fraternity brothers. Then he permanently immigrated to the United States in 1924. He worked on a dairy farm in Imperial Valley, California, for a year or two; near San Diego, he passed up an opportunity to buy land for the price of $1.00 per acre! He then moved north, holding the job of managing the six dairies at the Edson-Foulke ranch in Gazelle, California, from 1926 to 1937. His final position was Siskiyou County Administrator for the United States Department of Agriculture in Yreka, California, from 1937 to 1962. The striking thing about Hans's childhood, schooling, and career is that it was entirely in agriculture, farming; contrarian, he spent his whole life in an industry that most people in the twentieth century were leaving.

The final thirty years of his life were spent in retirement, initially in Yreka, and then in Las Vegas, Nevada. And, like Nils, Hans also made a return trip back to Skåne in 1964, for a visit, and perhaps lament the sale of the family estate.

Correspondence

After a separation of some forty years, Nils and Hans enjoyed a rather regular and good natured correspondence with one another in the 1960s and 1970s. While none of these letters remain for inspection, one amusing exchange has survived in the oral history.

In the 1960s Hans was aware of the news about apartheid in South Africa as well as the trial, conviction, and imprisonment of Nelson Mandela in 1962. At the same time Nils was cognizant of the civil rights movement in the United States, including the 1963 march on Washington, D. C., to protest racial injustice, where Martin Luther King gave his famous "I Have a Dream" speech.

In this context Hans, in one of his letters, asked Nils the accusative question, "Why don't you treat the black people in your country better?" And Nils, in his reply, asked Hans the equally piercing question, "Why don't you treat the black people in your country better?" The otherwise cheerful correspondence continued in spite of these tribal darts.

To be yourself in a world that is constantly trying
to make you something else is the greatest accomplishment.

Ralph Waldo Emerson (1803-1882)

3. HIGHER EDUCATION

Verna Rae Koepp Karstensson was my half-sister. She was the daughter of my mother, Iris Smith Koepp Karstensson, the only offspring of her first marriage to a man named Koepp. The Koepp marriage, for some unspoken reason, did not last long.

Born in 1925, Rae was some eight years old when her mother and Hans Karstensson were married in 1933. She was nine years older than my full-sister, Karna Karstensson, and fourteen years older than me, Lewis Karstensson. We were the Karstensson family initially of Gazelle, California, and then of Yreka 96097.

This piece is a recollection of an amusing episode in Rae's life. While the main features of the account are factual, some of the more minute details are likely fictional owing to a failing sixty-year-old memory supplemented by an imagination of the possible. All-in-all I suppose the account is seventy-six percent true.[*]

Background

Dad was raised in a well-heeled farm family in Sweden. He had a rather full education, the equivalent of a baccalaureate in agriculture. His post-gymnasium education consisted of three years of work in agricultural schools in Sweden, and one year of work at Purdue University in Lafayette, Indiana. Mom, on the other hand, was brought up in a rather poor family. She dropped out of school after the ninth grade in order to go to work to help support the family. Uneven in their formal education, they were nevertheless intelligent

---
[*] Leslie Susan Hance, Rae's daughter provided some useful details for this piece

and well-read. And they were insistent, adamant, that their children work hard in school to acquire the best possible education.

Rae graduated from Yreka High School in 1943, in the midst of World War II. She was a nearly straight "A" student, just a few grade points short of the now forgotten valedictorian and the also unremembered salutatorian. Dad and Mom would expect her to continue her education. However, since the war effort took precedence over personal preference at this time, patriotic Rae spent three years as another "Rosie the Riveter" doing her anonymous part for the cause of victory.

After the war the parents encouraged the daughter to return to school. So, in 1947, Rae applied for, and was granted, admission to the University of California, Berkeley. Entry into one of the top universities in the world was seen, in itself, as an important accomplishment.

At UC Berkeley

On the second Thursday in September, in a spirit of anticipation and adventure, the family crammed into Dad's car, a 1937 Ford Coupe, and headed for Berkeley. We initially went to the home of Uncle Ross and Aunt Verna Farnsworth in Oakland; Verna was one of Mom's younger sisters; there, after the long drive, we visited, supped, and spent the night.

The next morning, after breakfast, we set about the tasks of preparing Rae for her University life. First, we went to the registrar's office on campus where she signed up for her fall semester courses. Next we had to find the boarding house on Channing Way where she would be living, and move her personal things — clothes, comb, toothbrush, etc. — into her room. And after lunch we went to the bookstore to get the books, notepaper, and pencils needed for her classes. With the boring essential chores completed we did something fun; we all took the elevator up to the top of the Campanile to get a grand view of the campus and the surrounding bay area. Finally, we returned to the Farnsworth hotel for supper, and more conversation before retiring for the night.

Then, Saturday morning, we took Rae over to her new digs, said our goodbyes, and started the drive back to Yreka. Mom and Dad were satisfied that they had done all they could to prepare Rae for a productive semester, a successful start to her university career.

The semester progressed as expected. In letters and phone conversations Rae reported all going well. There was, she said, a lot of reading and writing in her English composition class, but she was enjoying the creative writing assignments in the class; the professor in her United States History class was an entertaining lecturer, made the dead subject somewhat interesting; College Algebra was teaching her that math was not her strong suit; and her Speech class involved preparing and delivering speeches, nervously, in front of discussion sections of the class. The classes were demanding, but she was managing to get passing grades on her exams, papers, and presentations.

Toward the end of the term, in December, the family was again excited, looking forward to Rae's returning home for Christmas break. Mom and Dad were interested in talking to her, face-to-face, at length, about her classes and grades, to see how she was faring in her first semester. Mom, anxious, took the bus down to Berkeley to meet Rae and bring her home.

Surprise

When mother and daughter met at the place on Channing Way, Rae opened a proverbial "Pandora's Box" and out sprang a huge, HUGE, surprise. She informed her mother that she was not going to school! She had not been going to school all semester! All the letters and phone conversations over the semester were fictitious, a charade! She had had enough of school! She did not want any more of it! She wanted to see the world!

Back in September, the week after she had enrolled, Rae withdrew from her classes, went to the University Employment Office, and filed an application for a job. Two skills she had mastered in high school were shorthand and typing; she could take a letter in shorthand and type it out in perfect form at an error-free rate of more than 80 words per minute. She had the skills to be an excellent stenographer and she knew it. She was hired immediately, and had been working all semester in the Physics Department at the University, doing correspondence and typing research papers, reports, and examinations.

Iris was shocked, stunned, at the news of her daughter's dropping out of school and going to work. She told Hans of the surprise in a phone conversation, that night. The two tried to get the daughter to see the importance of her education, persuade her to go back to school, but Rae would not hear of it, her mind was made up, and nobody was going to change it. There was nothing more that Iris and Hans could do to sway their daughter toward more schooling. After spending another day visiting Verna and Ross in Oakland, Iris returned home to Yreka via bus, sans Rae, who, of course, had to work.

The World

Rae did make good on her desire to see the world, or at least some of it. While yet employed in the Physics Department, she made inquiries about foreign service work with the United States Federal Government. She found that branches of the military, including the Army and Navy, hired civilians for service at military bases around the world. And some of this was stenographic work for which she was well qualified. She applied and was assigned. With only brief breaks Rae spent the decade from 1948 to 1958 in the service of the Navy and Army, overseas, as a civilian employee.

She had three tours of duty over the decade. The first assignment was in the Pacific, a two-year stint at the U. S. Navy base on Guam followed by a two-year stay at a base at Tokyo, Japan. The second excursion was a three-year obligation at the Army base at Wiesbaden, Germany. And the third tour was a return to Guam for a year followed by shorter assignments in Saudi Arabia, Lebanon, and finally at the National Security Agency in Washington, D. C.

Rae knew these assignments would not be all work and no play. She often partied with GIs after work, and went on sightseeing excursions on weekends and holidays. During her stay in Germany, in May 1953, she took a leave to tour Sweden and visit several of Dad's relatives including his two sisters, Selma and Clara. And it was during her second stay in Guam that she found time to cultivate a relationship with, and a short-lived marriage to, one Willard Thomas Hance, a union that produced the daughter, Leslie Susan Hance.

With her appetite for foreign travel sated, Rae returned home to Yreka in June 1959, with her two-year-old daughter, Sue, in tow. She spent the remainder of her professional career as Executive Secretary in the local branch of A. P. Giannini's Bank of America. Rae retired in 1987 and moved to Chico, California, to be near her daughter, Sue. She passed away in 1994.

In Sum

There probably is no moral to this story, but there may be a lesson. Rae certainly had ample mettle to do very well as a student at UC Berkeley, but that was not what she wanted. She wanted to travel and see, up close, other places in the world. And that is what she did. The lesson? In spite of the sound guidance of parents for their offspring, the damn kids, unlike other largely programmed animals in nature, often go their own way!

Doctor Pangloss was right in telling me
that all is for the best in this world....

Voltaire
Candide (1759)

4. FADER AND DAUGHTER

Hans Karstensson was the *fader*, father, old world, from Sweden. Karna Karstensson was the *dotter*, daughter, and my sister. Might have been Karna Hansdotter, but she was new world, child of California. The relationship between the two was traditional – steward to the novice, sage to the curious, guardian to the vulnerable femme fatale. The demeanor of the daughter was largely respect to the *fader* and obedience to reasonable parenting. However, there was the occasional civil disobedience for unreasonable governance. A memorable instance of the latter transpired in 1950 when Karna turned sixteen. Age sixteen was sweet for a variety of reasons, not least because of its importance as the year of passage, when the adolescent obtained her certificate of virtual adulthood, the driver's license.

Cruising the Drag

Cruising the drag was a frequent recreational activity of the youth in our home, the small town of Yreka. Cruising the drag was driving around town, usually down Miner Street from Gold Street to Broadway and then out Broadway and Main Street to the Diner at Brownie's gas station, and back again. Then repeating the same circuit perhaps a half-dozen times, stopping once at the Diner to have a Coke. This is how Karna and friends – Barbara Bryan, Sally Jeter, and others – spent an occasional Friday or Saturday night when there was nothing better to do.

One Friday evening shortly after she got her driver's license Karna and friends went cruising in the family car, a 1949 Ford Fairlane, two-door, 4-

speed, V-8. They cruised from eight to about ten o'clock. After having their satisfying portions of good fun – girl talk and flirting with boys, also cruising, – they went home.

The Mileage Problem

The morning after the ride Karna's *fader* inquired where she had gone. He had checked the odometer before and after the cruise and noticed that 36.8 miles had been put on the car. This, to the *fader*, was an excessive mileage, wasteful. Karna answered that she and her friends had gone nowhere, they had just driven around town, and around town, and around town. The *fader* concluded, out loud and in an accusative voice, that this wasteful driving was not proper. He saw this as an occasion, not only to thwart profligate behavior, but also to remind her that he, the *fader*, was yet the steward, and she was still the juvenile daughter, who needed to show obedience as well as greater parsimony behind the wheel.

Karna, affronted, saw the *fader's* response as disgraceful, an insult to her deserved respect, her independence, her honor. If the mileage was a bit excessive it was not a grave transgression. Besides the odometer insight revealed his prejudice, his inclination to question rather than trust, her ability to behave in a proper manner. This, she insisted privately to herself, was plainly arbitrary, today abusive, parenting.

The Solution

While the passage of time diminished the overt confrontation between *fader* and daughter, the difference remained festering in Karna's mind just beneath the conversation of the day. There had to be, she thought, a solution to the excessive mileage problem. The odometer, how does it operate? It records increased mileage when the car is moving forward. Is it possible that it would record decreased mileage when the car, in reverse gear, moved backward? The next time she and her friends went cruising they tested the proposition. And guess what? Backing up *did* decrease the mileage shown on the odometer. A clear solution to the excessive mileage problem was to put the car in reverse and back around town!

Thereafter, that is exactly what she did when she and her friends went cruising in the Karstensson Ford. She would spend an hour or so driving around town, as before, in the forward gears, and then at the end of the evening spend a half-hour driving in reverse on some of the town's less-traveled back streets. The result was apparently acceptable since the *fader* never again raised the mileage issue.

Postscript

This incident was widely known during Karna's years of cruising from 1950 to 1952. Nearly everyone in Yreka and the surrounding area knew of the episode, and laughed about it. Indeed, several people in town ran the odometer test on their own vehicles. While most of the tests produced the expected result of increased mileage driving forward and backward, a few cars yielded the contrary result of decreased mileage in reverse.

The affair is now forgotten. However, there does remain a monument of a sort to the event. The "legacy" for each graduating senior student in the class of 1952 at Yreka High School is recorded in the *White and Gold*, the school yearbook. Karna's Legacy therein: "Backing around town!"

And what did the *fader* think of the daughter's solution to the excessive mileage problem? Methinks he never knew of it.

It does not matter how slowly you go as long as you do not stop.

Confucius (551-479 BC)

5. HUMAN CAPITAL

W e television addicts find the flat screen interesting for reasons beyond the Golf Channel. For example, I am a fan of the Sunday night CBS news program, *60 Minutes*, although the current shows are something less than those of the past, concluded by the great Andy Rooney. Yet the shows still feature stories that I find either interesting or conducive to sleep, both results entertaining at my age.

One memorable piece aired on November 24, 2013. Anderson Cooper interviewed author, Malcolm Gladwell. The subject of the interview was Gladwell's then newly published book, *David and Goliath*.[*] The interview, interesting, seduced me into buying the book. And the volume turned out to be more than a good read – a read about a variety of situations in which seemingly ordinary people confront extraordinary challenges. One chapter, Chapter 4, a chapter on dyslexia, caught my attention for good reason. It had something profound to say about my personal stock of human capital or lack thereof.

Dyslexia

So what is dyslexia? Let me summarize a bit of Gladwell's description. The source of the disorder is in defective fetal brain development. The fully developed brain of a dyslexic has a shortage of grey matter, brain cells, in the occipital and/or parietal lobes of the brain. These are the sections of the brain

[*]Malcolm Gladwell, *David and Goliath: Underdogs, Misfits, and the Art of Battling Giants* (New York: Little, Brown and Company, 2013).

where visual, word recognition, and reading functions are processed. The disorder is, thus, the result of a maldeveloped brain.

The brain condition produces slow reading development in childhood years, labored reading in subsequent years, and a lifetime of sluggish reading ability and impaired reading comprehension. Then, of course, the ailment causes substandard performance in subjects requiring reading, like literature, the sciences, and social studies, that is, practically all fields of study.

And individuals afflicted with the disorder endure its distressing effects. Taking long periods of time to complete simple assignments, or leaving them only partly completed; finding oneself daydreaming, or doodling, or just sitting for long periods of time accomplishing little or nothing because the assignment is too difficult; and taking home report cards from school at the end of the term suggesting failure and little progress.

Dyslexia, in sum, is a deficiency of cell matter in the word processing regions of the brain which results in severe limitations in reading ability, and the consequent constrained performance in academic areas involving reading. Gladwell's chapter on dyslexia captured my attention because the descriptions therein resembled the difficulties I had in reading and my resultant deficient performance in elementary and high school.

My Dyslexia

While I have never been formally diagnosed with dyslexia, there is no doubt in my mind that I have some form of the disorder. So what I have to say here about my condition is neither clinical nor measured, but rather anecdotal, artifacts of my memory. And I believe I have sufficient storage capacity in my grey matter to underscore the claim that my memories are somewhere around ninety per cent correct.

My first impression that I had a problem was early on, probably when I was in the second grade in 1947 at the Grammar School in Yreka, California. I do have a vivid memory of sitting at my desk. The teacher, Mrs. Bryan, had given us a worksheet involving reading a simple one-paragraph story and answering questions about it. We were instructed to do the worksheet in class. While the other kids completed the work in about fifteen minutes, I was able to do only half the assignment before Mrs. Bryan collected our papers. Later that day my paper was returned to me with the comment printed thereon in big red letters, "WORK FASTER, LEWIS!" I knew I had a problem. I didn't know what the problem was, but I knew I couldn't do what was expected of me, what the other kids in the class were able to do with some ease. The next day we were given a similar worksheet to be completed in class. I knew I would again not be able to finish the assignment in the allotted time. So, I thought, "Why try?" Instead of doing the worksheet I did something fun; I turned the paper over to its blank side and drew an airplane. Well, this flight produced a parent-teacher conference. After the conference my Mom admonished me, "Listen to the teacher! Follow the teacher's instructions! You must try harder!" And at the dinner table that night my Dad's instruction was short, pointed, and stern, "Attend to business, Lewis!"

This was just the first of many disappointing episodes throughout my grammar school years from 1947 to 1953. Report card days were grim. The report card always told a tale of much failure and little success in reading, writing, and arithmetic. They were days of fateful questions, "What's wrong with Lewis? Why can't he get his work done? Why does he persist in being lazy?" And Dad, at the dinner table, would always repeat his short, pointed, and stern scold, "Attend to business, Lewis!"

My high school years, from 1953 to 1957, at Yreka High School, were not much different although I am sure Mom and Dad had, in these years, lowered their expectations of my academic achievement. I was almost always overloaded with work in nearly all my classes, work which I could only rarely complete. A few specific examples should suffice to illustrate the particular among my difficulties. In Mrs. Luedloff's English class, in addition to the daily classwork and homework assignments, we were required to read and submit a written book report each term; I completed this requirement by reading and reporting on, not the full length books that were assigned, but the *Classics Illustrated* comic versions of the books. Then, at my Dad's insistence, I took a year of Latin which was also difficult; the vocabulary, noun declensions, and verb conjugations were just more than I could memorize. And I was always behind in my work in my social studies, science, and math classes. At the open house in the spring term of my junior year, my United States History teacher, Mr. Ed Loudin, commented to my Mom, for good reason, "Don't send Lewis to college. He will not succeed at that level. Don't waste your money."

While my years in elementary and high school, thus, had an unpleasant side owing to my reading handicap, other facets of my life were not so dismal in these years. I was generally a happy kid who had many friends. I enjoyed playing sports and had some modest success in baseball and basketball. My best sport was tennis. My friends and I enjoyed the outdoor activities of skiing, hunting, fishing, and camping. I even enjoyed music, playing the trombone in band in the sixth, seventh, and eighth grades. While I was, yes, slow in reading music, I did learn to play rather well by ear. I even had a bit of success in one school setting. I spent the summer of 1955 living with my sister, Karna, in Berkeley where she was a student at the University of California. We had an apartment on Telegraph Avenue a couple blocks away from Sather Gate. While she took classes at UC, I enrolled in two morning classes – an English class and a crafts class – at Oakland Technical High School, commuting via municipal bus. I did well in both classes because I could keep up with the work of the relatively light course load. And I played pickup tennis matches at the UC courts in the afternoons. It was an altogether enjoyable summer.

A Conversation

Well, the lax standards at Yreka High School permitted my graduation in June 1957. And the also lenient admission standards allowed my entry into Humboldt State College in the fall term. One day in late June before the start of school in September, I had a resolute conversation with myself. In the exchange ME is me in a stern, insistent, voice; MY is myself in a submissive, agreeable, voice. The conversation went something like this:

ME: You know, we need to have a serious talk.
MY: I know.
ME: You have a lousy education! You are woefully ill prepared for college!
MY: I know.
ME: What do you want to do with your life? How do you intend to make a living? Do you want to spend your life digging ditches? Or would you rather do something in a more leisure line, something more interesting, in a profession less physical, less strenuous?
MY: Certainly the latter!

ME: Well then, you had better make up your mind to get serious in college, and work your derrière off in your classes! There will be no time for social life!

MY: Yes, I intend to work very, very, hard!

Thus was the conversation between me and myself.

The hard work took shape when the semester started. I, of course, attended classes and took careful lecture notes. Outside of class I found a quiet place, either at my desk in my dorm room or in the library, rewrote the day's lecture notes, and did the assigned readings carefully, often reading and rereading paragraphs over and over and over as necessary until their meaning was clear. And I put in long hours preparing for exams. Of the 168 hours in a week, I probably spent an average of 15 hours in class; then some 63 hours eating, sleeping, showering, doing laundry, etc.; and finally the remaining 90 hours studying with periodic short breaks. I was hell-bent on beating my reading handicap by putting in long, and focused, hours of study, work!

The Results

In retrospect, the work paid off professionally. I completed my BA degree in social science in 1962 and then did the fifth year of work to get my California General Secondary Credential. My career was initiated teaching history and economics classes at Marysville High School during the five years from 1964 to 1969. I found economics to be the more interesting discipline; its models were useful in examining individual behavior and public policy issues. So I went back to graduate school at Ohio University where I completed MA and PhD degrees in economic education. Thereafter, I had a quite satisfying career teaching economics – economic education, microeconomics, statistics, and history of economic thought – first at North Texas State University from 1975 to 1979 and then at the University of Nevada, Las Vegas, from 1979 to 2007. I am now Emeritus Associate Professor of Economics, in retirement, from UNLV.

I didn't really beat my reading disability in my thirty-eight year career of university level work. I just learned to live with it, both in graduate school and in my years of teaching economics. I just had to continue spending long, long, hours studying, doing my research, and preparing for my classes. But then, this was work that I found largely enjoyable.

Good Company?

In Chapter 4 of *David and Goliath*, Gladwell suggests a possible relationship between dyslexia and professional success. In support of this connection he points to a number of highly successful dyslexics: British billionaire Richard Branson, discount brokerage firm founder Charles Schwab, cellular phone businessman Craig Mc Caw, Jet Blue founder David Neeleman, Cisco CEO John Chambers, Kinko's founder Paul Orfalea, and Hollywood movie producer Brian Grazer with *A Beautiful Mind* among his credits.

And to Gladwell's list we can add: Actress Jennifer Aniston, environmental activist Erin Brockovich, astronaut Charles "Pete" Conrad Jr., King of Sweden Carl XVI Gustaf, Prince of Sweden Carl Philip, Crown Princess of Sweden Victoria (heir-apparent to the Swedish throne), inventor Thomas Edison, Governor of Colorado John Hickenlooper, and artist Pablo Picasso, among many many others.

I am tempted to lay claim to be among this good company of successful dyslexics. However, the claim, if granted at all, is slight. For I am a much lesser accomplished Eliab among these far-seeing Goliaths. And yet, I must say, in spite of my disorder, I am now catching up on the good reading of Cervantes, Dickens, Hemingway, Molière, Steinbeck, Twain, Voltaire, and a host of others, whom I was supposed to have read back in my high school and college years.

To be able to forget means sanity.

Jack London
The Star Rover (1915)

6. OH TANNENBAUM

We all have our Christmas memories, those happy or mundane, exhilarating or disappointing, humorous or serious, planned or spontaneous events enjoyed, flouted, or just tolerated in our Christmases past. A reminiscence of mine, ironically more indelible in my memory than perhaps any other, involved an instance of youthful absentmindedness.

I grew up in Yreka, California. At age sixteen I got my driver's license. From that point on, at least during my years at Yreka High School and in my undergraduate years at Humboldt State College, when home on break, it was my job to run various driving errands for the family. I was, you might say, the on-demand family courier. So each year, at Yuletide, it was my job to go out into the wilds of Siskiyou County to retrieve the family Christmas tree.

It was December of 1955 around St. Lucia's Day. I took off, alone, one afternoon in the family car, a 1949 Ford Custom two-door sedan, to get the tree. I went south of town, up Greenhorn Road some fifteen miles to a point between Mill Creek Road and the Mt. Vernon Mine, a closed mine where you could still see the piles of copper tailings with the greenish hue. South of the road was a mixed stand of oak, ponderosa pine, and fir trees of varying sizes. Here, I would be able to find the sort of tree we liked – a healthy, six-foot, fully branched, largely symmetric douglas fir. And, in those days, it was not illegal for an individual to harvest a Christmas tree on public land.

I pulled off the road, parked the car, opened the trunk. Oh hell! I had neglected to check for the axe before leaving the house. We had always used an axe to fell our tree. Well, this time, I had forgotten the axe. There was no axe in the car!

I pondered my dilemma for a bit. My ponder yielded two possible ways of dealing with the problem.

I could drive back home, get the axe which was no doubt in the garage at the house, and then drive back to the forest site to commence my search for the tree. This option seemed on the cumbersome side since it would have involved a thirty-mile round trip before initiating the tree hunt.

The other alternative involved using a different, somewhat unconventional, tool, or set of tools, to bring a tree down. I had my dad's Winchester 32 Special, Model 94, rifle and a box of shells, twenty cartridges, in the car. Family lore held that dad had won the rifle in a punchboard game in 1929. And I had my fairly sharp pocket knife in my pocket. My strategy would be to shoot at the base of the tree so as to splinter its trunk. Once pulverized by the bullets, I could then finish off the tree, as it were, by cutting the remaining splinters with my pocket knife.

This latter tack seemed workable. So I grabbed the gun and ammo, and proceeded on my hunt for an attractive fir tree. Well, I found the tree, used all twenty rounds to splinter the trunk, and whittled the remaining connections until the tree was completely severed from its stump. I then took the tree to the car, loaded it in the trunk, and hauled my bag limit home.

The rest of the story is on the ordinary side. In the garage, I sawed off the splintered base, mounted the tree on a stand, and took it into the living room corner where we had always placed our Christmas tree. Over the next day or two mom, my sister, and I decorated the tree. We put on the strings of variously colored lights. We put on the ornaments of different sizes, shapes, and colors. Then we had to put on the damn silver colored tin tinsel, the same damn tinsel saved and used year after year. And mom, with the best of intentions, insisted that we put the damn stuff on very carefully.

Humor keeps us alive. Humor and food.
Don't forget food. You can go a week without laughing.

Joss Whedon

7. SURVIVAL OF THE UNFITEST

When we were kids we occasionally went on what we called survival outings. These were weekend camping trips where we tried to live off the land. The gear we took on these sojourns included fashionable clothes and boots, a sleeping bag, a canteen, some old cooking and eating utensils, some salt, a knife, a 22 caliber rifle with a box of shells, a fishing rod and tackle, and cigarettes – all conveniences that could not easily be found in the wild, in nature. Perhaps, deep down, we wanted to try out the hunter-gatherer way of life of some of our ancestors. Or maybe we were just out to be survivalists, before that disorder came into fashion.

While the details of most of these outings have either been forgotten or are blurry memories, one of the trips stands out, remains vivid, in my mind. One afternoon in June 1953, or thereabouts, my mom, the late Iris Alameda Smith Karstensson, took a carload of us kids down to a flat on the Shasta River some ten miles northwest of Yreka. The load included Dennis Bennett, Larry Hornberger, Richard Keyes, Ted Peters, perhaps an unremembered other, and myself. We must have been thirteen or fourteen years old. Mom dropped us off at a wide spot in the road on Friday and said she would return to pick us up at the same place the following Sunday afternoon. That would give us two full days to fend for ourselves in the wilds, rather like Henry David Thoreau at Walden Pond, although we made no attempt to build a cabin.

That afternoon we selected a more-or-less level elevated area overlooking the river for our camp. We dropped our gear there. We then proceeded to go hunting, in a libertarian way without plan, in all different directions. A couple of us went down to the river to hunt bull frogs. The others struck out for the higher country in various directions above our camp hunting for big game, like squirrels and rabbits. Birds were off limits, not in season. After a couple hours of traipsing around we all sauntered back to camp, each with the same unproductive tale. We didn't see a thing. None of us even got off a shot. So the grand take on the first afternoon was nothing. And we went to bed hungry.

The next day, Saturday, was much the same. We went hunting again, and fishing, without result. It was as if the fish and game saw us coming and decided to vacate the territory for the weekend. We also went foraging for blackberries, raspberries, and pine nuts. I think we may have gotten a few nuts, but we found no ripe berries. The grand take on the second day was next to nothing. And we went to bed again, even more hungry.

The final day, Sunday, was different. When we didn't think things could get worse, they did. In addition to our hunger, the day started out with a cold drizzle and progressed to a cold rain. We did not have weatherproof gear. As the day wore on, we became increasingly soaked and cold and uncomfortable and hungry. We did the best we could to seek warmth and shelter, huddling next to a fire under a grove of willow trees down by the river. But the willow branches and leaves, dripping rain water, provided only illusory shelter and discouraged the fire to the point where it provided more smoke than warmth. Yet we all remained cloistered in the mock shelter.

That is, all but one of us. Richard Keyes was perhaps the most persistent and hardy of our lot. And it is probable that he was the hungriest among us, at least on that day. Midmorning he decided to make one last pass through the hills above the camp in search of food. Shortly after he left, we heard a shot coming from his direction just beyond a ridge. Soon we saw Rich coming back over the crest and walking down the hill toward us. As he approached, our eyes were fixed on what he was holding in his hands. His right hand was toting his gun. Then, dangling, head down, from the left hand was a dead chicken, a rooster. Either the chicken had strayed a mortal distance from the farm that happened to be on the other side of the hill, or Rich's hunger had caused him to stray too close to the farm. Whatever the case, we were hungry, and we now had food.

In short order, the rooster was gutted, plucked, and put in a kettle over the fire. We had arranged rocks on either side of the fire pit to support the pan over the flames. We added wood to the fire. We watched the bird cooking. We turned the bird in the pot every few minutes. We salivated at the cooking bird.

After about forty-five minutes the chicken looked cooked, done. The pan was taken off the fire, the rooster removed, and cut up. I was given a drumstick. I expected my first bite would yield a hot, tender, tasty chicken nugget of the dark meat sort. What I found in this bite was a gastronomic shock, a tough piece of poultry, hot on the outside, but still cool on the inside. I immediately spit out the bit off piece of leg. I inspected this chunk as well as the bitten into section of the drumstick. While appearing cooked on the outside, both were a glistening purple on the inside. The coolness, toughness, and color all suggested poultry tartare, chicken yet raw, and repulsive to my discriminating palate. The noxious state of the chicken leg decimated my appetite. I now had a preference for starvation over raw, or now even cooked, rooster! While I thus gave up on consuming the leg, my companions put their similarly raw pieces of chicken back, not in the pot but into the fire, burned the hell out of them, and ate the resulting chunks of carbon.

After a couple more hours of suffering the soaking cold and continuing hunger, mom came to pick us up. She transported each of my fellow-travelers-in-the-wild home and then made the final stop at our house. At home, in my appreciated dry home, and my appreciated warm home, my appetite returned. I wolfed two big peanut butter sandwiches and washed them down with a Pepsi.

This survival outing suggested a corollary to Darwin's dictum of natural selection. It is possible for even the unfit to survive if there is only a loaf of bread, a jar of peanut butter, and a Pepsi nearby.

I followed an ostensibly lame turkey over a considerable part of the United States one morning, because I believed in her and could not think she would deceive a mere boy, and one who was trusting her and considering her honest. I had the single-barrelled [sic] shot-gun, but my idea was to catch her alive....

More than once, after I was very tired, I gave up taking her alive, and was going to shoot her, but I never did it, although it was my right, for I did not believe I could hit her; and besides, she always stopped and posed, when I raised the gun, and this made me suspicious that she knew about me and my marksmanship, and so I did not care to expose myself to remarks.

I did not get her, at all. When she got tired of the game at last, she rose from almost under my hand and flew aloft with the rush and whir of a shell and lit on the highest limb of a great tree and sat down and crossed her legs and smiled down at me, and seemed gratified to see me so astonished.

Mark Twain
"Hunting the Deceitful Turkey" (1906)

8. SAGEBRUSH GEESE

The late Stanley Hornberger was a fine man and an accountant under the employ of the U. S. Forest Service at the headquarters of the Klamath National Forest on the second floor of the Warrens Building on Broadway Street in Yreka, California. He was also the father of my good friend and hunting companion, Larry Hornberger.

One day in the vicinity of October 1952, Stanley and his colleague, Ted Simpson, took Larry and me on a hunting trip to Butte Valley. If my dating is correct Larry and I were thirteen years of age at the time of this adventure. We arose early in the morning and drove the sixty-some miles on Highway 99, county road A12, and Highway 97 to the wide spot in the road called Macdoel. From Macdoel we drove a mile or two west on Meiss Lake Road to the Shoemaker Farm.

The Shoemakers rotated potato, barley, and wheat crops on the fields of their several hundred acre farm. We were interested in hunting in the barley or wheat stubble fields where flocks of ducks and geese would feed in early morning hours. We were given permission to hunt in the Shoemaker fields by virtue of the absence of "No Hunting" or "No Trespassing" signs on their land; their fields would have been posted with such signs if they had not wanted hunting thereon.

Stanley dropped us kids off at one stubble field while he and Simpson went on to another field. Larry and I were dressed in fashionable clothing and boots appropriate to the occasion. We loaded our shotguns, and headed for a dry irrigation ditch on one side of the field which we used as a blind overlooking the stubble. Larry had his Winchester 12 gauge, pump shotgun, and a duck call, while I had my Browning 20 gauge, automatic shotgun, and no duck call. We settled into the ditch, smoked a cigarette, and waited for sunrise.

We stayed in the ditch for an hour or so after daylight. We could see flocks of ducks and geese flying off in the distance, but nary a duck or goose came over us in range, or landed in our field. When we grew tired of waiting for birds to come to us we thought we should make an effort to go to the birds. So we set out walking across our field looking for birds that may be feeding on neighboring grounds.

Soon we found what we were looking for, a large flock of birds feeding in an area beyond our grain field. We crouched down, crawled closer, and looked carefully at the assemblage. We were sure they were geese, strange looking geese, a species different from those with which we were already familiar. And they were behaving strangely. They were feeding, not in grain stubble, but in an adjacent range of untilled largely bare sandy soil where half-dead bunch-grass, stunted sagebrush, and scrawny jackrabbits seemed to be barely eking out an emaciated living. It was hardly an ecosystem of nourishment. But these birds were feeding on something in that uninviting habitat. And they were geese, we were sure of it. And we were hell-bent on hunting them down.

So we got on our bellies and crawled stealthily toward the birds. When we got within range, or what we thought was within range, some thirty yards away from the flock, we rose up and fired two or three rounds at the birds. We got no birds. The only result was that the birds got up and flew thirty yards further away from us and resumed their feeding, or preening, or posing, or whatever. The birds were otherwise unfazed. And we repeated this iteration of sneaking up on the birds, shooting at the birds, and watching the birds fly thirty yards further away, several times with the same unrewarding result. While the birds did not seem to mind our little game, we found it rather annoying.

Finally, after the seventh or eighth iteration, Larry's dad snuck up behind us and fired the question, "Why are you kids shooting at those Sandhill Cranes?" Well, that killed our hunt, on that day, at the Shoemaker Farm. As Larry and I walked back to the car to begin our trip home in humiliation, the flock of deceitful geese went on with their feeding, preening, posing, and probably chuckling, under their breath, at the naïveté and the marksmanship-not of their assailants.

Being young is a fault that diminishes daily.

Swedish Proverb

9. HOLIDAY ON ICE

I suppose it was somewhere around Christmas 1956. We were sixteen or seventeen year old high school kids living in the Northern California town of Yreka. Dennis Bennett, Larry Hornberger, Gary Plunkett, and I drove on a very cold day, in Plunkett's old green very cold, no heater, 1948 Chevy, the sixty-some miles up to Butte Valley to do some goose hunting.

It was not the sort of day for a successful hunt. For some reason we got a late start from Yreka and didn't get to our destination, the Macdoel area, until late morning. So we missed the ordinarily more fruitful early morning hunt when we could either set out decoys in a stubble field and wait for hungry birds to fly in to them, or crawl up on birds already on the ground feeding in a field. Furthermore, it was a clear, cold, bright sun, blue sky, high visibility day. It was a day where we could see birds a long way off, but also a day where the birds could see us from a long way away. The advantage in such high visibility situations is normally for the wily birds that are very good at avoiding easily, and not so easily, detected hunters. In spite of the odds against our success we were determined to do some hunting.

Past ventures had afforded some useful information on the fall and winter season habits of waterfowl. We knew that ducks and geese, with some little variation, spent their early mornings feeding in stubble, grain, or alfalfa fields. Then their late mornings and afternoons were spent resting, preening, conversing, and otherwise socializing on nearby lakes or streams or wildlife refuges, areas affording a measure of safety from hunters. It was now late morning so the birds would soon be taking flight, moving in large flocks from field to water. We, thus, decided to set up at Meiss Lake (Meiss rhymes with geese), a large body of water just west of the town of Dorris, and then wait for the birds to come to us.

We drove over to the southern edge of the lake. Our gear consisted of our shotguns, shells, three gunny sacks of flat cardboard silhouette Canada goose decoys, and cigarettes. And at the edge of the lake we found a couple scrawny tumbleweeds that might be fashioned into a pervious blind. The lake, except for a patch of open water in its middle, was frozen over, solid. We walked perhaps a half mile out on the ice with our gear. We set out the decoys, probably two or three dozen. We knelt down on the empty gunny sacks behind the scrawny tumble-ble weeds. Facing east toward the decoys, we were ready for the birds.

To our amazement, the birds came, and came, and came again. They came from the north, from the east, from the south. High in the sky at first, the flocks fell like fluttering pieces of paper toward a point just south of us, then set their wings to regain their flight control, and finally flew north toward our position at a low, well in range, altitude. They apparently mistook our decoys as a real flock of friends, and perhaps saw us homo sapiens as little more than mounds of dirt sustaining plants that were now dry weeds. And if Bennett or Hornberger used a goose call, as they were sometimes inclined to do on these occasions, their conversation was apparently friendly and inviting for a change, not the least bit offensive to the birds.

The first flock came over our decoys right in front of us. We shot the legal three shells each. Hit birds fell out of the air. We celebrated for a moment. We reloaded, crouched down again, and waited for the next flock. The second flock came over our decoys right in front of us again. We shot the legal shells each again. Hit birds fell out of the air again. We celebrated for a moment again. We reloaded, crouched down once more, and waited for another flock. The third flock came over our decoys right in front of us again. We shot the legal shells again. Hit birds fell out of the sky again. We celebrated for more than a moment this time.

This goose shoot lasted no more than an hour. And at the end of it we were pretty sure we were over the limit in birds. The limit in those days was three birds each. So the collective limit for the four of us was twelve birds. When we counted up the geese on the ice we found twenty-two dead pacific white-fronted, speckle breast, geese. We were ten birds over the limit!

At this, we knew we needed to pick up our gear and birds, and get the hell off Meiss Lake before a game warden happened on the scene. Thus, with some considerable urgency we stuffed most of the geese into two of the gunny sacks, and crammed the decoys into the third sack. Bennett and Hornberger each dragged a sack of geese back to the car, albeit with some difficulty. They were only barely able to maintain traction on the ice while towing sixty pound sacks of geese. Plunkett dragged the somewhat lighter sack of decoys to his car. I carried the guns and a couple unsacked geese to the vehicle. Finally, off the ice at Plunkett's Chevy, we stuffed the birds and gear into the trunk and ourselves into the car, for the cold, no heater, return drive home.

Back in Yreka we apparently made a stop at the Bennett house on Lane Street where the goose hunt was recorded on film in Dennis's backyard. The hunters and the hunted appear in the photo on the next page.

The Meiss Lake Goose Hunt: The Hunters and the Hunted

Pictured (left to right): Lewis Karstensson, Larry Hornberger, Dennis Bennett, Gary Plunkett.

Photograph courtesy of Gary Plunkett.

Two things are infinite:
the universe and human stupidity;
and I'm not sure about the universe.

Albert Einstein (1879-1955)

10. CRIME AND PUNISHMENT

The adolescent years are well known as a time of experimentation where youth test the boundaries between approval and disapproval, between regions of social acceptability and of tribal taboo. It is the universal process wherein the uncivilized become civilized, or probably just somewhat less uncivilized. We, the uncivilized 1950s cohort who grew up in the Wild West, in Yreka, California, were immersed in this process and forced into conformity by sundry pressing means. This piece is an occasion to remember two ventures into boundary testing, actually boundary invasion, into low level crime and punishment. The first event occurred on a ranch south of Gazelle. The second happened on marsh land north of Montague. This account, I would guess, is somewhere around seventy-five percent accurate.

The Gazelle Episode

The Maxwell ranch was just south of Gazelle in Shasta Valley. The ranch held two parcels of land, one on the east side of old Highway 99 and the other on the west side of the Highway, with the ranch house just off the thoroughfare on the west side facing east. The acreage on the west side of the highway was given over to growing alfalfa hay; the east side acreage was patches of permanent pasture and scrubland covered with sagebrush and grass suitable for light livestock grazing. It was a cattle ranch. On the scrubland, as well, were a couple depressions that collected rain and runoff water forming ponds that attracted waterfowl. And wherever waterfowl were drawn we were attracted.

It was perhaps a day in October 1956. Dennis Bennett, Larry Hornberger, Richard Keyes and I went hunting out in Shasta Valley. From Gazelle we drove a mile east on Louie Road and then a couple miles south on Slough Road. This put us in the vicinity of a pond on the Edson-Foulke ranch where we had permission to hunt and had done so frequently. We were hoping to get a shot or two at birds at this location. But, alas, there were no fowl on or around the mere on this day.

In our thus found lull we probably smoked a cigarette while contemplating our next move. Looking around, we noticed a flock of Canada Geese, honkers, circling and then landing off in the distance to the west, perhaps a mile away, on the Maxwell ranch.

Now the Maxwell place was off limits to us. It was posted with "No Hunting or Trespassing" signs on every tenth fence post. We not only did not have permission to hunt thereon, the posters instructed us to stay off the property. So we climbed through the barbed-wire fence onto the forbidden land and started walking toward the point where we had seen the geese.

Some distance into our hike we saw a man on horseback riding toward us. As he approached it became clear who he was. It was old Glen Maxwell, the owner of the property we were on, illegally, illegally on the two counts prohibited by the posters. We were clearly trespassing since we were on his land, and the guns we were toting were a dead giveaway that we were hunting. We braced ourselves for the inevitable reprimand.

In an agitated voice, Maxwell informed us who he was, asked that we identify ourselves by name, and suggested that we were not welcome on his property. We politely listened to what he said, complied submissively with his request for our names, and nodded agreement with his every word. We knew our only chance to get out of this predicament less, rather than more, scathed was to resign our lots to the mercy of old Maxwell.

But then in an unexpected reversal, a somewhat sympathetic Maxwell said that a flock of geese, the flock we had seen in the first place, had landed on one of his ponds in the direction we had been walking. Then he offered a proposal. If we would agree to vacate his land afterword, and not come back, he would let us try to hunt down that flock of geese. We thankfully agreed.

We hunted those geese without success. In retrospect, my guess is that Maxwell let us pursue that flock knowing that he would get a good laugh out of our failure. There was nothing around the pond to use as cover to sneak up on the birds – no ditch, no vegetation, no buildings. So three of us took up positions on the north and east sides of the pond while the fourth approached the pond from the south so as to scare the birds over the positioned shooters. Well the wily honkers took off to the west. And while we got nary a shot, Maxwell had his laugh. Birds outsmart kids again!

The next day, the very next day, Fred Benton, Ted Peters and I went hunting out in Shasta Valley. From Gazelle we drove a mile east on Louie Road and then a couple miles south on Slough Road. This put us once again in the vicinity of the pond on the Edson-Foulke ranch where we hoped to see some birds. But once more there were no birds at said loch.

However, might those geese be back at the Maxwell pond today? For some reason, grounded in nothing more than hope, we thought it unlikely that the old man would be out there patrolling his ranch on his horse again today. He would likely be elsewhere doing other things. With this expectation in mind we climbed through the barbed-wire fence onto the forbidden property again and headed toward the Maxwell pond.

Well, you know what happened! Halfway into our trek, there appeared on the horizon a man on horseback. We knew who the man was this time, even at a considerable distance. We ran as fast as we could back toward the car. The escape was unsuccessful. When he caught up to us old Maxwell gave us, particularly me, a well-deserved verbal thrashing of the most severe sort. I don't know about my companions, but I never ventured onto the Maxwell property again, ever.

The Montague Incident

We had nothing better to do one morning in December 1956. So Dennis Bennett, Larry Hornberger, Richard Keyes and I put our shotguns in the car and headed into Shasta Valley in search of birds. We spotted some ducks landing in a slew north of Montague, just south of Shelley Road, between Ager Road and Willow Creek Road.

I think we noticed that the land was posted, "No Trespassing." But we didn't know who owned the land, and we didn't see anyone around enforcing the prohibition so we parked the car on the side of Shelley Road, climbed through the barbed-wire fence, guns in hand, and headed toward the slew. We hunted for perhaps an hour, got no birds, probably smoked a cigarette, and then headed back to the car.

Well, back at the vehicle, we found a surprise. There was an official-looking cream-colored folded paper on the driver's side of the windshield, tucked under the wiper blade. An official-looking cream-colored paper on a windshield is rarely a good thing. And sure enough, it was a Court Order, doubtless written out and placed on the windshield by a duty-bound neighborhood Constable.

It was a summons to report to the Siskiyou County Clerk of Courts for the purpose of scheduling an appearance to answer the charge of trespassing on private property. We complied with the Order. In due course we were instructed to report to the Montague Judicial District Court on an appointed day and time, say Friday, March 15th, at 4 o'clock *post meridiem.*

We went to court in the company of our parents. The Montague courthouse turned out to be the residence of Laird M. Johnstone, the Montague Judicial District Judge, and the courtroom was the Judge's bedroom. His Honor was clearly afflicted with an illness of a serious sort.[*]

We were greeted at the front door by a sturdy rural woman, the Judge's nurse who doubled as the court reporter and bailiff as justice may have required. Our cases were considered individually in alphabetical order – first Bennett, then Hornberger, then Karstensson, and finally Keyes. The first defendant was ushered into the Judge's bedroom with the others instructed to wait in the living room. When the first criminal was dismissed, the second was marshaled into the courtroom, then the third, and then the fourth. Our cases were thus serially adjudicated by a bed-ridden Judge propped up to a sitting position by large bulky white pillows fluffed up against a cherry-wood backboard, his legs covered with a heavy white quilt.

We each pled guilty placing our respective fates in the hands of the Magistrate. Our pronounced sentences were the same. We were assessed $25 fines. The fines were paid by our parents, but we were required to reimburse them the same full just amount in a reasonable period of time. And we were put on a six month probation with the condition that if we managed to stay out of trouble during this trial period the misdemeanor charges would be stricken from our records. I believe we repaid our parents, and kept any further trouble that we may have gotten into under wraps, out of sight of the Judge.

---

[*] James B. McAdams, "The Court History of Montague & Tablerock," *The Siskiyou Pioneer* (Yreka, California: Siskiyou County Historical Society, 1986), Vol. 5, No. 9, pp. 69-71. According to McAdams, "Judge Johnstone was in failing health for a number of months before his death [on April 8, 1957] and he was obliged to hold court in his bedroom. His home was located at Webb and 9th Streets in Montague."

Terminus

These unpleasant episodes brought to light, in a most glaring way, the following obtuse rules of civility. First, it is really difficult, if not impossible, to outrun a man on a horse. And, second, if you are ever inclined to trespass onto posted property, it is not a good idea to park your car in plain sight.

A well regulated Militia,
being necessary to the security of a free State,
the right of the people to keep and bear Arms, shall not be infringed.

Second Amendment (1791)
Constitution of the United States

11. GUN CONTROL

G rowing up in the Wild West, in Yreka, California, in the 1950s was ad-
venturous, at times downright dangerous. It is amazing some of our
numbers, afflicted with severe adolescence, did not take up residence in jail,
or worse, in the local cemetery, on account of our risky antics. This piece is an
occasion to remember two incidents involving the Hornberger brothers, Dale
and Larry, at the time fourteen and fifteen years of age, respectively, and two
guns, a 30-06 rifle and a 12-gauge shotgun. While I did not witness either
event, I was privy to accounts at the time, as well as versions in the din of oral
history down the years. This account is, I believe, at least eighty-eight percent
accurate in its main details.

The Rifle

The Hornberger house was located near the northwestern edge of town,
at 700 Knapp Street. Humbug, the hill, was practically in the back yard. And
the Hornberger bedroom, the slumberia of Larry and Dale, was something of
a recreational center for the mob of teenagers that hung out together during
their years at Yreka High School. The gang included the Hornbergers, Dennis
Bennett, Fred Benton, Richard Keyes, Mike Nunes, Bob Wolgamot, myself,
and any number of other drifters who occasionally wandered in. Here we
played poker and smoked cigarettes on Saturday nights. And there was nearly
always a running chess game. Here we had conversations about victory and
defeat in sports, about our hunting and fishing adventures, and about our fe-
male conquests and fears. And here we planned our occasional starvation

camping trips, efforts to live off the land, which were always unsuccessful although not fatal.

The bedroom, located at the back end of the one-car garage, was of a middling size housing twin beds and a raised built-in clothes closet that extended into the garage and over the hood of the car parked therein. A large window on the back wall at the head of the beds gave a panoramic view of the northern foothills off in the distance, of Elm and Pioneer Streets to the near northwest, and of a rental cottage in the neighbor's backyard to the nearby northeast. In the corner of the bedroom next to the head of Larry's bed, stood a couple guns and a fishing rod with a tackle box on the floor.

One August afternoon in 1954 Larry took the Winchester, Model 54, Mauser bolt-action, 30-06, and went coyote hunting up in the foothills. Yes, coyote hunting with a 30-06, the equivalent of going after a fly with a snow shovel! Returning home, sans coyote, he put the gun back in its place in the corner by his bed. Larry was always very careful in handling firearms. He removed the cartridge from the barrel chamber of the gun, pushed it down into the spring-loaded magazine, and closed the bolt without chambering a round. Even though there was a full complement of four cartridges left in the magazine, there was no chance of accidentally firing the gun without a shell in the breech.

Some days later Larry's brother, Dale, had something of a Walter Mitty moment in the bedroom. He imagined himself a combatant in the recently concluded Korean War, revived only in his mind. An invading force of North Koreans was at the northern border of Yreka poised to overrun the city. An enemy sniper was holed up in the neighbor's cottage looking out a window at the ready. It was up to Lieutenant Dale Hornberger, crack sharpshooter in the U. S. Army infantry, to take out the sniper. Hornberger picked up his Army issue 30-06, aimed it at the cottage window, and pulled the trigger, "CLICK!" This first shot missed its target. A second shot was necessary to do the job. Hornberger worked the bolt, took aim again, and resqueezed the trigger, "KA-BOOM!"

The shot kicked Dale's shoulder, hard, and jolted him out of his dream. His mom, Louise, in the kitchen on the other side of the house, heard the explosion and came scurrying into the bedroom wondering what in the world had happened. Dale, in shock, told her in a quivering voice, that he was pretending to defend the city from a North Korean invasion and the gun accidentally went off sending a bullet out of the bedroom and into the neighbor's cottage. This explanation put Louise into shock! The bedroom window was unscathed only because it was open, but the window screen, blown out of its frame, was lying outside, on the ground, a short distance from the house sporting a bullet hole and powder burns.

But what about the cottage? An old man lived there! Was he home? Was he frightened? Was he angry? Was he hit and unconscious? Or, God forbid, was he killed by the bullet, dead? Neither Dale nor Louise could go over to the cottage to check on the old man. What they might discover was too awful, too terrible, too horrid, unbearable. Son and Mother were paralyzed by the situation, immobile in the bedroom.

A short time after the shot was fired and the paralysis had set in, a composed Larry came home and was told what had happened. He immediately went over to the cottage, knocked on the door, peered in the windows, and otherwise nosed around, and concluded that the old man was not home. He, however, did see a fresh bullet hole on the left side of the window frame at the front of the cottage.

When the moment became teachable at the dinner table that evening, the Hornberger parents, Stanley and Louise, instructed Larry to completely unload all guns in the house from then on, and Dale was asked to choose fantasies producing less alarming results. The Hornbergers never discussed the incident with the neighbors; it was just too painful, too embarrassing, to talk about. And the neighbors never mentioned the episode either; perhaps they, too, like the old man, were not home at the time of the shot. The incident was brought to closure a week or so later when Dale, shoulder still bruised and sore, noticed that the bullet hole in the window frame had been patched and painted over.

The Shotgun

Larry Hornberger and his dad, Stanley, were usually game for going hunting for whatever happened to be in season. They found themselves so inclined on one gloomy December afternoon in 1954. Driving south on Highway 99 into Shasta Valley they angled over to the West Side Road between Grenada and Gazelle. There they spotted a flock of white-fronted geese, specks, feeding in one of the snow-covered stubble fields along the road.

Stan and Larry were strategic hunters in the sense that they carefully thought through a shoot before carrying it out. The plan this time was simple. Stan would drop Larry off by a dry irrigation ditch at the north-west corner of the field, and then drive down to the south end of the field. Larry would crawl in an easterly direction some fifty yards on his hands and knees in the ditch, in snow and mud, to a point roughly half way across the north end of the field. Then Stan would walk east and then north from the south-west corner toward the flock in the middle of the field. The birds, seeing Stan approaching from the south, would take flight toward the north and go over Larry within range. The expectation was an easy bag of two birds.

Why two birds? The gun Larry was using on this day was a 1904 vintage L. C. Smith, two-trigger, side-by-side double-barrel, 12-gauge shotgun. It was unlikely there would be sufficient time to reload, to get more than two shots off. Incidentally, Stan was armed with a Western Field, pump-action, 12-gauge shotgun, with a 32-inch Browning barrel.

With the plan fixed and the guns loaded, the action commenced. Larry crept down the ditch, took up his position on his knees, and waited for the birds to be flushed in his direction. Stan did his thing, walking toward the geese. The birds took off and flew, as expected, directly toward Larry. When they were nearly overhead Larry rose up and sighted up the rib between the barrels toward a target goose. He squeezed the front trigger exploding the shell in the right barrel. Instead of seeing a goose fall out of the sky Larry saw a butterfly land on the left barrel of his gun! He then aimed the gun at a second goose and pressed the back trigger discharging the shell in the left barrel. Again no bird fell to the ground. The geese flew on, frightened, but unscathed, in a north-easterly direction toward Charlie Drummond's refuge.

With the action concluded, Larry took stock of the situation. He pulled his gun down and looked it over. What he saw was astonishing! The end of the right barrel was splintered with strands of steel bent outward from its center! The rib was bent upward, in a slight arc, away from both barrels! But the left barrel remained largely unaltered in its original form and position. What had happened? Well, in slithering down the snow-lined ditch Larry had apparently plugged the right cylinder with snow and mud. Pressure from the discharged shell caused the barrel itself to explode and splinter out. And the bug Larry saw? There were, of course, no butterflies working that frozen stubble field in December! Perhaps it was an amalgam of mud and snow and gunpowder blown to the rib and congealed in the shape of an insect of the Lepidoptera Order. Or maybe it was a vision somehow projected from the butterfly in his stomach. Or maybe just a figment of his imagination. In any event, it was fortunate, indeed, that the only injury in the ditch on that day was the one inflicted on L. C. Smith, the gun.

Conclusion

If you should ever find yourself in the company of the Hornberger brothers and their guns, the perilous Hornberger brothers, take cover! And yet this may be unwarranted, overcautious advice. After all, gun accidents do occasionally produce survivors.

All parents damage their children. It cannot be helped.
Youth, like pristine glass, absorbs the prints of its handlers.

Mitch Albom
The Five People You Meet in Heaven (2003)

12. SOME ENCHANTED EVENING

Prank, antic, caper, chicanery, escapade, exploit, foolery, gag, gambit, high jinks, hoax, lark, monkeyshine, ploy, practical joke, ruse, scheme, shenanigan, trick. These are things of first-order interest to most boys in their juvenile years. Few things in the life of an adolescent are more satisfying, more exhilarating, than taking part in crafting and executing a clever prank, and then enjoying the profound sense of accomplishment that comes with the success of the caper. Conversely, few things in a young man's life are more embarrassing, discomforting, shameful, than being a party to a gag gone bad, and then suffering the subsequent humiliation.

This appreciation of the prank comes to mind in reference to an evening nearly sixty years ago in which I and a number of my male high school classmates tried to carry out two such capers, one an utter failure, the other a lifting success. I want, herein, to go back to that evening, to recount the events as best I remember them. The reader must bear in mind that this account is what *I* remember, and while I am certain of the accuracy of the large features of the evening, the memories of others involved in the adventure may well produce versions different from this account in some of the very small details, the trivial particulars.

Background

It was Wednesday, October 31, 1956. Halloween! A dance was scheduled for that evening, from seven to ten o'clock, at the old gymnasium at Yreka

High School. The dance was doubtless promoted by the school and civic authorities to provide, first, a wholesome activity for the youth of the town and, second, something that would keep mischief-prone adolescents off the streets and out of trouble. And it was early in the evening because it would not be wise to keep the juveniles up too late on a school night. The plan of the adults was for the kids to have some chaperoned fun at the dance, but then go home for the night and be rested for school the next day. The kids' plan, our plan, was otherwise. It seemed the perfect evening for a bit of fun of a different sort, some foolery. And our inclination was not so much in the direction of following the wishes of the authorities as in attempting to evade, even scoff at, the locals in power.

The First Prank

Early in the evening, before the dance, we were driving around town, "cruising the drag," we said in our day. Cruising the drag was the ritual of driving around town, usually down Miner Street, from Gold Street to Broadway, and then south on Broadway and Main Street (Highway 99) to Brownie's gas station and back again, over, and over, and over. The ritual probably celebrated some rite of passage, perhaps demonstrating the independence that came from having recently acquired a driver license.

The "we" who were cruising the drag included Dennis Bennett, Larry Hornberger, John Wilson, one or two other unremembered classmates, and myself. Hornberger claims not to have been involved in the first prank of the evening. But I believe he was. He was always involved in our pranks, frequently the instigator. He probably just doesn't remember, what with his old age and all. And even if he wasn't involved in this one, literally, he certainly was, figuratively, to the extent that he would have been with us if he had known of our planned mischief.

I don't remember whose car we were cruising. It is possible that we were in my pre-owned and pre-wrecked 1941 Studebaker President which required as much crankcase drain as gasoline to run. It was well known in town for its sprung-chassis tilt to the left and down in front, and the thick blue smoke contrail it produced when roadborne.

Whatever the car, one of our number suggested that it might be neat – neat was the word for cool or rad or bad in those days – it might be neat to try to remove a gate from the chain-link fence surrounding the house and yard belonging to Lester Newton. Mr. Newton, at the time, was the Siskiyou County Probation Officer. It was his job to check up on sundry parolees and other delinquents, making sure they were not again going too far astray of the law. He was an authority figure, and to us a prominent one, and his removed gate, in our minds, would be a worthy prize, a large trophy, although we never gave thought to what we would do with it once it was liberated from the fence and in our possession.

The Newton house was located on the northwest corner of the junction of Jackson and Gold Streets. There were two gates from which to choose. One was on the Jackson Street side leading to the front door of the house. The other was on the Gold Street side near the back door. We thought it wise to choose the one in close proximity to the back of the house since the costumed little ones would likely be trick-or-treating at the front door.

So in the dark of early evening we drove up to the Gold Street gate, got out of the car, and went over to the gate to inspect its connection to the fence, to see how the two were attached, and to see how one might be de-tached from the other. Just as we were commencing the inspection the back-porch light came on, the back door to the house opened, and out stepped Lester Newton, looking straight at us. We did not stay around to have even the slightest conversation. We, instead, piled back into the car and departed the scene, very quickly.

This attempt stifled, we returned to our cruising down Miner Street and up Broadway again. Perhaps we honked our horn at other cruisers, or stopped for small talk with other riders. We, also, no doubt, chatted among ourselves, contemplated our next move. At some point in time, perhaps a half-hour after our first assault on the Newton gate, we decided to attempt the heist a second time. Lester, we imagined, would now be occupied in servicing the little trick-or-treaters at his front door. Moreover, our single-minded quest for the "Holy Grail" led us to believe that Newton would not expect us to approach his prop-erty a second time, or if he did, the Lord would see to it that he looked the other way.

Thus, on faith alone, we again drove south on Gold Street from Miner Street toward the gate. When we got there, before we could even get out of the car, we were shocked by the appearance of the white Yreka City police car, right in front of us, with its single pulsating red warning light on. So much for the Lord's assistance. The police car had come out from behind the house on Jackson Street and turned left onto Gold Street stopping right in front of us. Out of the driver side of the car, and toward us, came Hank Watson, the Chief of Police. Lester Newton followed from the passenger side of the car. I am sure some conversation ensued, but I don't remember much of it. I, however, do recall one line, the command Hank Watson issued in a low stern voice, "You boys go down to City Hall, right now!"

We, in this instance, did submit to authority. We drove down to City Hall on Main Street followed by the Chief and the Probation Officer in the police car. As we drove we wondered about our fate, with trepidation. When we arrived at City Hall, Watson instructed us to be seated on the hard wooden benches just inside the door of the City Clerk's Office in front of the counter where citizens came to pay their water bills. Watson and Newton went into the adjacent Chief's Office and closed the door. We resumed wondering our fate with more trepidation. We discussed the matter in hushed tones. We expected the worst: To be held overnight in jail and suffer the indignity of being escorted home the next morning, in full daylight, in the Police Car; or to endure the shame of being driven home by our parents and, once there, scolded and given some domestic punishment. We waited, and waited, and waited, for what seemed like an eternity, but was probably something less than twenty minutes.

Finally, Chief Watson came out of his office to pronounce sentence. In the same stern voice he said: "If you boys will go to the dance, go straight home after the dance, and not cause any more trouble, we will let you go."

Those words fell on elated, no, ecstatic, ears. In tones polite and submissive each of us said, or thought: "Thank you Sir, yes Sir, we will go to the dance and then straight home, Sir. We won't cause any more trouble, Sir." At that, we got back into the car, drove from the City Hall up to the old gym, and went to the dance.

I don't remember what we did at the dance. We may have danced, or not. We may have watched others dance, or not. We may have just stood on the sidelines sulking about our botched gate heist. Whatever we did was apparently unmemorable. The dance was certainly the least impressive event of the whole evening. But I am pretty sure we stayed at this unimpressive event until the chaperones proclaimed the dance over and told us we had to leave.

The Second Prank

The events after the dance are a good deal clearer in my mind because these were the circumstances surrounding the second prank of the evening. Leaving the dance together, again in an unremembered car, were Bennett, Hornberger, Wilson, perhaps another classmate, and myself. We were supposed to go straight home, but that was not appealing. Our appetite for chicanery was not yet satisfied. So we, once again, drove around contemplating what mischief we could venture into before going home.

Suddenly, in the flash of the proverbial light bulb, the dazzling idea came to one of us that we should retrieve a portable toilet from one of the construction sites on the edge of town, transport it to one of the main intersections in town, and put it upright in the middle of the junction. In doing this, we thought we would be providing a valuable service to the community, erecting a civic statue. Except this statue, unlike the metal or stone effigies of city fathers which only dogs found useful, would actually be a functional convenience for the municipal citizenry!

It was unanimous, we all agreed that we should provide this important public service. First, we needed a truck in which to haul the monument. So we went over to Dennis Bennett's house on Lane Street to borrow his dad's old, beat up, Chevy pickup. Then, we took the pickup truck up to the new housing division on Knapp Street, west of North Oregon, where houses were being built, and loaded up the most attractive and durable porta-potty we could find. Next, we hauled the bathroom to the confluence of Miner and North Oregon Streets, between the Elks Club and the Fire House, west of Soldane's Liquor Store and the palindromic Yreka Bakery, and east of the Carnegie Library. Finally, we unloaded and centered the monument in the intersection, facing east, so that the front door would catch the morning sun. With the statue in place, a tribute was observed: John Wilson opened the door, entered the facility, sat down on the throne, and majestically christened the monument, so to speak, as the rest of us bore witness in rapt constipation. With our civic duty finished, our appetite for a successful shenanigan satisfied, we went home.

Afterword

In the day or two that followed this hallowed evening, nothing was ever said of the failed gate heist, nothing was remembered of the dance, but there was a good deal of talk in town about the outhouse in the intersection. But, then, shortly after the event the one-holer disappeared from the crossroads. City authorities, apparently not appreciating our aesthetic contribution, probably ordered it returned to the construction site.

Today, over a half century later, perhaps the only evidence of the porta-potty episode is that in the memories of the involved delinquents. And yet there is a lingering, nagging, remnant in my memory that the occasion was recorded by a notice, or picture, in the *Siskiyou Daily News* a day or two, or week, after the affair. But then this remnant may be simply an artifact of my airy imagination.

Then God said, "Let us make humankind in our image according to our likeness, and let them have dominion over the fish...."

Genesis 1:26 (c. 500 BC)

13. THE LURE

In retirement I am occasionally, if not frequently, inclined to think about trivial, foolish things. An episode of this folly centers on what I recently mined from a conversation with Larry Hornberger concerning his creation, the Hornberger lure, which he offered up in all seriousness, indeed, with considerable enthusiasm.

Larry and I were originally connected as, sometimes sane sometimes crazy, members in the Class of 1957 at Yreka High School, and have only recently relapsed into conversations over our shared and unshared pasts. Now Larry, not an understatement, seems to have turned out to be something of a naturalist. Impressive, he spent a career of nearly forty years as a civil engineer with the U. S. Forest Service in California and Montana. More impressive, he walked, in 2009 at age seventy, the some 220 mile stretch of the Pacific Crest Trail from Yosemite to Mt. Whitney, the John Muir Trail, surviving the 21 days mostly on fish that he caught along the way. And most impressive, in 2011 he managed to drive the 3,000 mile roundtrip between Santa Barbara, California, and Craig, Colorado, in a pre-owned Ford pickup vintage 1990 overused with a *Grapes of Wrath* style camper shell, for an entirely unsuccessful five-day muzzle-loader elk hunt in the Rockies, surviving on food other than the aimed-at elk. These details are merely to the point of suggesting Hornberger's credentials to tackle tackle innovation.

So what is this Hornberger lure? Begin with an oblong plastic torpedo bubble with eyes on each end. The eye on the small end is attached to the fishing line that goes down the rod to the reel. Connected to the eye on the large end of the bubble are three menu items. The first is a treble hook, size 8 or 10, with two blue stripes painted with an indelible marker on the aforementioned bubble, an assemblage presumably representing a blue dragonfly to the fish. The second item is a two-foot length of leader going to a size 16 or 18 green mosquito fly. And the third item is another two-foot leader with a size 16 or 18 black gnat fly attached to its end. (All these components are available at your neighborhood Bass Pro, Trout Pro, and Salmon Pro Shops.) To this three-item menu is added a final ingredient, a seasoning of a sort, doubtless the *pièce de résistance* to the fish: dabs of WD-40 oil on the tackle. It is an axiom of quite a number of anglers that WD-40 is largely fish oil, apparently tasty, or at least not repulsive, to caught fish! Finally, an application of silicone dry fly treatment to the lure assures its buoyancy in water.

And how is the lure used? Cast the assembled bait far out into the water. Straighten the line with a couple cranks of the reel. Let the ripples in the water disappear. Twitch the apparatus repeatedly for a bite, that is, bring the assembly in about five feet and let it settle for a bit, then repeat. By the second twitch you will have a trout or three on the line. If not, try again, and again, and again!

This, then, is the Hornberger lure and its use. It may not be such a trivial, foolish, thing. Indeed, it may well be the greatest invention to come from the Class of 1957 at YHS!

FOUR CRONIES

The following characters, friends really, figured more-or-less centrally in one or more of the herein recounted adventures.

The late Dennis Bennett was raised in Yreka, California, and attended local elementary and high schools. He went on to a fifteen-year career of pitching in professional baseball, seven years in the major leagues mostly with the Philadelphia Phillies and the Boston Red Sox. He was on the 1967 Red Sox "Impossible Dream Team" that won the American League Championship. After his baseball career Dennis operated the Yesterday's Plaza, a shopping and restaurant complex in Klamath Falls, Oregon. Following Sam Malone, he tended bar at the City Club in the Plaza. He also spent time road hunting deer, elk, antelope, ducks, geese, and pheasant, even occasionally on the Klamath National Wildlife Refuge.

Larry Hornberger, a product of Yreka, earned a B.S. degree in civil engineering at Sacramento State College. He then had a thirty-seven year career with the United States Forest Service in Montana and Southern California, in the Montecito National Forest. Larry now resides in Goleta, California, where he invests in hunting tags, invents fishing lures, and even goes hunting or fishing, when he remembers his gun or rod.

Gary Plunkett, a native of Grenada, California, and product of Yreka High School, earned a B.S. degree in civil engineering at Chico State College and became a licensed civil engineer in California. He was serially Director of Public Works for the city of Sausalito, Colusa County, and Tehama County. Gary now resides in Florence, Oregon.

The late John Wilson, another product of Yreka, founded and managed for some years the Golden Movement Emporium, a really large architectural antique dealership featuring products wanted primarily among the rich in the Beverly Hills, Hollywood, Santa Monica areas of Southern California. The products he vended included Roman marble bathtubs, exotic sinks, classical Greek and Roman columns, statuary, fountains, stone mantels, artistic wood, glass, and iron work, and antique outhouses. Wilson, then, went into real estate development, out of the country, in Costa Rica, hawking property in one Buena Vista Lake Arenal Resort Community.

THE AUTHOR

Lewis Karstensson was raised in the small northern California town of Yreka. He attended the local elementary and high schools. He received a B.A. degree in social science at Humboldt State College after which he taught history and economics at Marysville High School from 1964 to 1969. He then earned M.A. and Ph. D. degrees in economic education at Ohio University. Thereafter his career, from 1975 to 2007, was spent as professor of economics first at North Texas State University and then at the University of Nevada, Las Vegas. Since 2007 Karstensson has spent his retirement reading classics, writing a little, and watching old episodes of *Cheers*, *M*A*S*H*, and *Paladin* on Netflix. And he watches the Golf Channel. He even plays some golf. Like H. Richard Greene in the TV ad for a nutrition shake, "I'm terrible at golf. But I'd like to keep being terrible at golf for as long as I can."

CPSIA information can be obtained
at www.ICGtesting.com
Printed in the USA
FSOW03n2044010917
38308FS